Love
on the Cross

RICHARD GARRARD is Suffragan Bishop of Penrith in the Anglican Diocese of Carlisle. He has been a Priest in the Church of England for nearly 35 years, working in Inner London and East Anglia before moving to the North West. Adult education and spiritual direction are a major theme in his ministry. He is married to Ann who is an artist. They have two children, a son who is a Priest and a daughter who works in theatre.

Love
on the Cross

Reflective Services
for the forty days of Lent,
based on the
Gospel of Matthew

RICHARD GARRARD

First published in 1995 by
KEVIN MAYHEW LTD
Rattlesden
Bury St Edmunds
Suffolk IP30 0SZ

ISBN 0 86209 739 8
Catalogue No 1500037

Front cover:
Detail of the Estouteville Triptych, Flemish School 14th Century
Reproduced by kind permission of the Courtauld Institute, London

Edited by Alison Sommazzi
Cover design by Graham Johnstone and Veronica Ward
Typesetting and Page Creation by Louise Hill
Printed and bound in Great Britain.

CONTENTS

Introduction   5

Day   1   Ash Wednesday   8
Day   2   The First Thursday   10
Day   3   The First Friday   12
Day   4   The First Saturday   14
Day   5   The First Monday   16
Day   6   The First Tuesday   18

Day   7   The Second Wednesday   20
Day   8   The Second Thursday   22
Day   9   The Second Friday   24
Day   10   The Second Saturday   26
Day   11   The Second Monday   28
Day   12   The Second Tuesday   30

Day   13   The Third Wednesday   32
Day   14   The Third Thursday   34
Day   15   The Third Friday   36
Day   16   The Third Saturday   38
Day   17   The Third Monday   40
Day   18   The Third Tuesday   42

Day   19   The Fourth Wednesday   44
Day   20   The Fourth Thursday   46
Day   21   The Fourth Friday   48
Day   22   The Fourth Saturday   50
Day   23   The Fourth Monday   52
Day   24   The Fourth Tuesday   54

Day   25   The Fifth Wednesday   56
Day   26   The Fifth Thursday   58
Day   27   The Fifth Friday   60
Day   28   The Fifth Saturday   62
Day   29   The Fifth Monday   64
Day   30   The Fifth Tuesday   66

Day	31	The Sixth Wednesday	68
Day	32	The Sixth Thursday	70
Day	33	The Sixth Friday	72
Day	34	The Sixth Saturday	74
Day	35	The Sixth Monday	76
Day	36	The Sixth Tuesday	78
Day	37	The Seventh Wednesday	80
Day	38	Maundy Thursday	82
Day	39	Good Friday	84
Day	40	Easter Eve	86
Resurrection		Easter Day	88
Resurrection		Easter Monday	90
Acknowledgements			93

INTRODUCTION

Lent has forty days
– for the time Jesus spent in the desert before his ministry began,
– and one day for each year the Jewish people travelled the desert.

Christians today use Lent as a time for thought, fasting and reflection, seeking to know God more deeply, and to gain strength to live in the way of Jesus.

St Matthew wrote at a time when nearly all the eyewitnesses of Jesus's life had disappeared from the earth. He realised that the new church's leaders needed a reliable source of teaching material. Sifting and editing, he drew together a powerful tool to help later believers – like us – to grow to maturity in their life of faith.

USING THIS BOOK

Preparation

This book is primarily for groups that meet together and pray, whether in church or in smaller less formal gatherings. It may serve for as few as two people, or even as a personal devotion in the home or on retreat, or whenever you can find time to pray. It is designed to be used reflectively slowly with ample time for thought and prayer. The leader of the group will need to prepare carefully so that the words that are given can be shared with meaning and reverence. Haste is the enemy of prayer.

I suggest that the users of this book find a quiet place with minimum likelihood of disturbance.The members of the group can share the leading and the readings between them . . . But do remember the slow reflective tempo that brings the opportunity for private reflection as well as spoken words. Each day's service needs about fifteen minutes, and longer if the readings are taken as starting points for discussion.

THE ORDERS OF READINGS AND PRAYERS

The readings put Biblical passages beside non-biblical material to stimulate new insights and new way of focusing on God. On each occasion the readings are followed by an invitation to consider them with these key words:

PICTURE	the scene
PONDER	its meaning for you
PRAY	about it, in your own words as well the printed ones
PROMISE	to act on your prayers if they call you to action

The Prayer section includes thoughts for private as well corporate prayer. Remember to allow time for this. The Response sections which open and conclude each service have been printed in bold and medium type to encourage one person to lead and others to respond.The leader of these orders of prayer has a delicate task, but it is very rewarding. To minister to others gives a deeper grasp of one's own faith and understanding.

May the words in his book help you to find words to praise, thank and make requests to God, who loves to listen to our prayers.

RICHARD GARRARD

THE ORDERS
OF
READINGS AND PRAYERS

O Lord, open our lips:
to praise you, our Lord and our Christ.

FIRST READING   Te Deum vv 8-13

You Christ are the King of glory:
the eternal Son of the Father.
When you became man to set us free:
you did not abhor the Virgin's womb.
You overcame the sting of death:
and opened the kingdom of heaven to all believers.
You are seated at God's right hand in glory:
we believe that you will come and be our judge.
Come then Lord and help your people:
bought with the price of your own blood.
And bring us with your saints:
to glory everlasting.

SECOND READING   Matthew 16:13-23

Now when Jesus came into the district of Caesarea Philippi, he asked his disciples, 'Who do people say that the Son of Man is?'

And they said, 'Some say John the Baptist, but others Elijah, and still others Jeremiah or one of the prophets.'

He said to them, 'But who do you say that I am?'

Simon Peter answered, 'You are the Messiah, the Son of the living God.'

And Jesus answered him, 'Blessed are you, Simon son of Jonah! For flesh and blood has not revealed this to you, but my Father in heaven. And I tell you, you are Peter, and on this rock I will build my church, and the gates of Hades will not prevail against it. I will give you the keys of the kingdom of heaven, and whatever you bind on earth will be bound in heaven, and whatever you loose on earth will be loosed in heaven.' Then he sternly ordered the disciples not to tell anyone that he was the Messiah.

From that time on, Jesus began to show his disciples that he must go to Jerusalem and undergo great suffering at the hands of the elders and chief priests and scribes, and be killed, and on the third day be raised. And Peter took him aside and began to rebuke him, saying, 'God forbid it, Lord! This must never happen to you.'

But he turned and said to Peter, 'Get behind me, Satan! You are a stumbling block to me; for you are setting your mind not on divine things but on human things.'

PICTURE – PONDER – PRAY – PROMISE

PRAYER

Lord Jesus the Christ,
saviour of the world:
thank you for this time of Lent.
Make us clearer in faith,
and more ready to follow your truth,
that others may see in us
your victory over sin and death.

Thoughts for private prayer

Thank God for Jesus our suffering Lord.

Pray to understand him more deeply.

Pray to share in his death to sin and his resurrection glory.

We are dead to sin:
and alive to God in union with Christ Jesus.

O Lord, open our lips:
to praise you, our Lord and our Christ.

FIRST READING   Charles Everest (1814-1877)

Take up thy cross, the Saviour said,
if thou wouldst my disciple be;
deny thyself, the world forsake,
and humbly follow after me.

Take up thy cross then in his strength,
and calmly every danger brave;
'twill guide thee to a better home,
and lead to victory o'er the grave.

Take up thy cross, and follow Christ,
nor think till death to lay it down;
for only they who bear the cross
may hope to wear the glorious crown.

SECOND READING   Matthew 16:24-28

Then Jesus told his disciples, 'If any want to become my followers,
let them deny themselves and take up their cross and follow me.
For those who want to save their life will lose it, and those who
lose their life for my sake will find it. For what will it profit them if
they gain the whole world but forfeit their life? Or what will they
give in return for their life?

'For the Son of Man is to come with his angels in the glory of his
Father, and then he will repay everyone for what has been done.
Truly I tell you, there are some standing here who will not taste
death before they see the Son of Man coming in his kingdom.'

PICTURE – PONDER – PRAY – PROMISE

PRAYER

God of mercy and love,
we thank you that, in following Christ,
we begin to live the life of heaven
whilst still in time and space.
Make us faithful to his calling,
this day and every day.

Thoughts for private prayer

Pray for those whose lives are full of pain and weariness

Pray for your own death to selfishness.

Thank God for the strength to live in fellowship with Jesus.

We are dead to sin:
and alive to God in union with Christ Jesus.

O Lord, open our lips:
to praise you, our Lord and our Light.

FIRST READING

The cosmos we take as our own, will never be ours.
The greatest delusion of all: to think we possess.
The universe laughs in our face: 'preposterous pride!'
She answers each fixing of truth with ten questions more.
The more we believe that we know, we understand less.

Climb up the mountain of thought, the track ends in ice.
Quarry for laws that will last, and they will be changed.
Make poems that struggle for truth, they soon blow away.
Then look for the Christ who is real, the unity starts:
the God who became one of us, the end of the search.

SECOND READING   Matthew 17:1-8

Six days later, Jesus took with him Peter and James and his brother
John and led them up a high mountain, by themselves. And he
was transfigured before them, and his face shone like the sun, and
his clothes became dazzling white. Suddenly there appeared to
them Moses and Elijah, talking with him.

Then Peter said to Jesus, 'Lord, it is good for us to be here; if you
wish, I will make three dwellings here, one for you, one for Moses,
and one for Elijah.'

While he was still speaking, suddenly a bright cloud
overshadowed them, and from the cloud a voice said, 'This is my
Son, the Beloved; with him I am well pleased; listen to him!' When
the disciples heard this, they fell to the ground and were overcome
by fear.

But Jesus came and touched them, saying, 'Get up and do not be
afraid.' And when they looked up, they saw no one except Jesus
himself alone.

PICTURE – PONDER – PRAY – PROMISE

PRAYER

We thank and adore you
Jesus, God's own beloved Son:
before you terror and darkness are done away;
help us to look to you in living our lives in this world.

Thoughts for private prayer

Pray for those who have no faith.

Pray to be stronger in faith.

Thank God for Jesus, who has made God truly known.

Our eyes are fixed on Jesus:
the pioneer and perfecter of faith.

O Lord, open our lips:
to praise you, our healing Lord.

FIRST READING   Psalm 130:1-6

Out of the depths have I called to you, O Lord;
Lord, hear my voice;
let your ears consider well the voice of my supplication.
If you, Lord, were to note what is done amiss,
O Lord, who could stand?
But there is forgiveness with you;
therefore you shall be feared.
I wait for the Lord, my soul waits for him;
in his word is my hope.
My soul waits for the Lord,
more than the night-watch for the morning.

SECOND READING   Matthew 17:14-21

When they came to the crowd, a man came to him, knelt before him, and said, 'Lord, have mercy on my son, for he is an epileptic and he suffers terribly; he often falls into the fire and often into the water. And I brought him to your disciples, but they could not cure him.'

Jesus answered, 'You faithless and perverse generation, how much longer must I be with you? How much longer must I put up with you? Bring him here to me.' And Jesus rebuked the demon, and it came out of him, and the boy was cured instantly.

Then the disciples came to Jesus privately and said, 'Why could we not cast it out?'

He said to them, 'Because of your little faith. For truly I tell you, if you have faith the size of a mustard seed, you will say to this mountain, 'Move from here to there,' and it will move; and nothing will be impossible for you.'

PRAYER

We have so little faith, O Lord;
yet our needs are very deep:
help us to know our weakness,
so we shall learn to have faith in your strength.

Thoughts for private prayer

Pray for those in despair.

Pray for those in the grip of sickness in body and mind.

Pray for the leaders of the nations
that they may work together in faith and trust.

Thank God that he shall overcome all lack of faith and every evil.

In the depth of despair:
we find the life of faith in Christ Jesus.

O Lord, open our lips:
to praise you, the God of love.

FIRST READING   W. Walsham How (1823-1897)

It is a thing most wonderful,
almost too wonderful to be,
that God's own Son should come from heaven,
and die to save a child like me.

And yet I know that it is true:
he chose a poor and humble lot,
and wept, and toiled, and mourned and died
for love of those who loved him not.

And yet I want to love thee, Lord:
O light the flame within my heart,
and I will love thee more and more,
until I see thee as thou art.

SECOND READING   Matthew 18:1-7

At that time the disciples came to Jesus and asked, 'Who is the
greatest in the kingdom of heaven?'

He called a child, whom he put among them, and said, 'Truly I
tell you, unless you change and become like children, you will
never enter the kingdom of heaven. Whoever becomes humble like
this child is the greatest in the kingdom of heaven. Whoever
welcomes one such child in my name welcomes me.

'If any of you put a stumbling block before one of these little
ones who believe in me, it would be better for you if a great
millstone were fastened around your neck and you were drowned

in the depth of the sea. Woe to the world because of stumbling blocks! Occasions for stumbling are bound to come, but woe to the one by whom the stumbling block comes!'

PICTURE – PONDER – PRAY – PROMISE

PRAYER

Father of Creation,
we are the children of your love:
teach us a child-like trust
set free of childishness;
and a love of others
healed of jealousy;
grant us mature humility
and growing faith in you.

Thoughts for private prayer

Pray for children everywhere,
especially those deprived of love and care.

Pray for care agencies seeking to help families.

Thank God for his love of his children.

Pray to grow more aware of God's love for you.

We are God's children:
we walk in the light of his love.

O Lord, open our lips:
in praise of your loving kindness.

FIRST READING   Psalm 23

The Lord is my shepherd;
I shall not be in want.
He makes me lie down in green pastures
and leads me beside still waters.
He revives my soul
and guides me along right pathways for his name's sake.
Though I walk through the valley of the shadow of death,
I shall fear no evil;
for you are with me;
your rod and your staff, they comfort me.
You spread a table before me,
in the presence of those who trouble me;
you have anointed my head with oil, and my cup will be full.
Surely your goodness and mercy shall follow me
all the days of my life,
and I will dwell in the house of the Lord for ever.

SECOND READING   Matthew 18:10-14

'Take care that you do not despise one of these little ones; for I tell you, in heaven their angels continually see the face of my Father in heaven. What do you think? If a shepherd has a hundred sheep, and one of them has gone astray, does he not leave the ninety-nine on the mountains and go in search of the one that went astray? And if he finds it, truly I tell you, he rejoices over it more than over the ninety-nine that never went astray. So it is not the will of your Father in heaven that one of these little ones should be lost.'

PICTURE – PONDER – PRAY – PROMISE

PRAYER

Father of Creation,
we adore and praise your love of all that you create;
teach us to love as you love us, and to persist in loving.

Thoughts for private prayer

Pray for those whom you find it hardest to love.

Pray for those who have no one to love them.

Pray for those without love in times of crisis.

Thank God for his love made known in Jesus.

The Lord is our shepherd:
there is nothing we can lack.

O Lord, open our lips:
to praise your forgiving love.

FIRST READING   Thomas Benson Pollock (1836-1896)

Love that caused us first to be,
love that bled on Calvary's tree,
love that draws us lovingly,
teach us to forgive.

Love that knows that we have failed,
love whose hands we too have nailed,
love who on the cross prevailed,
teach us to forgive.

By the mercy we have known,
by the grace we did not earn,
heal our hatreds when we burn,
teach us to forgive!

SECOND READING   Matthew 18:15-22

'If another member of the church sins against you, go and point
out the fault when the two of you are alone. If the member listens
to you, you have regained that one. But if you are not listened to,
take one or two others along with you, so that every word may be
confirmed by the evidence of two or three witnesses. If the
member refuses to listen to them, tell it to the church; and if the
offender refuses to listen even to the church, let such a one be to
you as a Gentile and a tax collector.

'Truly I tell you, whatever you bind on earth will be bound in
heaven, and whatever you loose on earth will be loosed in heaven.
Again, truly I tell you, if two of you agree on earth about anything
you ask, it will be done for you by my Father in heaven. For where
two or three are gathered in my name, I am there among them.'

Then Peter came and said to him, 'Lord, if another member of the church sins against me, how often should I forgive? As many as seven times?'

Jesus said to him, 'Not seven times, but I tell you, seventy-seven times.'

PICTURE – PONDER – PRAY – PROMISE

PRAYER

God of infinite mercy,
we thank you for your merciful love for us;
may we whom you have forgiven learn to forgive
and be reconciled with those we fear, despise and hate.

Thoughts for private prayer

Pray for any people who you feel to have hurt and wounded you.

Pray for the leaders of nations, and communities,
that they may learn to forgive and be forgiven.

Pray for the healing of hatred and suspicion between races,
religions and all persecuted and their persecutors.

By the mercy of God:
may we show mercy to others.

O Lord, open our lips:
to praise you, the God of love.

FIRST READING

Father and Mother of endless creation,
maker of gender, woman and man,
giver of sexual passion and pleasure,
life-sharing, love-making,
deep in life's plan.

Grant to your children made in your image,
wisdom to honour these gifts of your grace,
gratefully sharing your work of creation;
spirit and body may
passion refine.

Let your deep instincts implanted within us
clear our confusions and teach us to live;
as you have made us so help us to hallow
body and soul in the
light of your love.

SECOND READING   Matthew 19:1-12

When Jesus had finished saying these things, he left Galilee and
went to the region of Judea beyond the Jordan. Large crowds
followed him, and he cured them there.

Some pharisees came to him, and to test him they asked, 'Is it
lawful for a man to divorce his wife for any cause?'

He answered, 'Have you not read that the one who made them
at the beginning "made them male and female," and said, "For this
reason a man shall leave his father and mother and be joined to his
wife, and the two shall become one flesh"? So they are no longer
two, but one flesh. Therefore what God has joined together, let no
one separate.'

They said to him, 'Why then did Moses command us to give a
certificate of dismissal and to divorce her?'

He said to them, 'It was because you were so hard-hearted that Moses allowed you to divorce your wives, but from the beginning it was not so. And I say to you, whoever divorces his wife, except for unchastity, and marries another commits adultery.'

His disciples said to him, 'If such is the case of a man with his wife, it is better not to marry.'

But he said to them, 'Not everyone can accept this teaching, but only those to whom it is given. For there are eunuchs who have been so from birth, and there are eunuchs who have been made eunuchs by others, and there are eunuchs who have made themselves eunuchs for the sake of the kingdom of heaven. Let anyone accept this who can.'

PICTURE – PONDER – PRAY – PROMISE

PRAYER

O God of wisdom and love,
in an age of confusion and doubt,
may we find the clear light of your grace
to guide and refine our powers of human love.

Thoughts for private prayer

Pray for those who cannot love.

Pray for those who seek love by sexual promiscuity.

Pray for people who suffer sexual abuse.

The eyes of the Lord are on those who respect him:
on those who trust in his love.

23

O Lord, open our lips:
let our lives proclaim your praise.

First Reading   Charles Wesley (1707-1788)

O Thou who camest from above,
the fire celestial to impart,
kindle a flame of sacred love
on the mean altar of my heart.

There let it for thy glory burn,
with inextinguishable blaze,
and trembling to its source return,
in humble prayer, and fervent praise.

Jesus, confirm my heart's desire
to work, and speak, and think for thee;
still let me guard the holy fire,
and still stir up the gift in me.

Ready for all thy perfect will,
my acts of faith and love repeat,
till death thy endless mercies seal,
and make my sacrifice complete.

Second Reading   Matthew 19:16-26

Then someone came to him and said, 'Teacher, what good deed
must I do to have eternal life?' And he said to him, 'Why do you
ask me about what is good? There is only one who is good. If you
wish to enter into life, keep the commandments.'
    He said to him, 'Which ones?'
    And Jesus said, 'You shall not murder; you shall not commit
adultery; you shall not steal; you shall not bear false witness;
honour your father and mother; also, you shall love your
neighbour as yourself.'
    The young man said to him, 'I have kept all these; what do I still
lack?'

Jesus said to him, 'If you wish to be perfect, go, sell your possessions and give the money to the poor, and you will have treasure in heaven; then come, follow me.' When the young man heard this word, he went away grieving, for he had many possessions.

Then Jesus said to his disciples, 'Truly I tell you, it will be hard for a rich person to enter the kingdom of heaven. Again I tell you, it is easier for a camel to go through the eye of a needle than for someone who is rich to enter the kingdom of God.'

When the disciples heard this, they were greatly astounded and said, 'Then who can be saved?'

But Jesus looked at them and said, 'For mortals it is impossible, but for God all things are possible.'

PICTURE – PONDER – PRAY – PROMISE

PRAYER

O Lord, you gave yourself for us;
help us to give ourselves to you.

Thoughts for private prayer

Praise God for the riches of his creation
and the good things we enjoy.

Pray that all that you have may be used for him and for his glory.

Pray for those besotted by possessions and the lust for more.

Pray for those who are starving and enslaved by poverty.

Pray that each may care for others,
that the world may know the love and the justice of God.

If any would be first:
let them be last and servant of all.

O Lord, open our lips:
to praise you in spirit and in truth.

First Reading   Psalm 19:7 and 9-11

The law of the Lord is perfect,
and revives the soul;
the testimony of the Lord is sure
and gives wisdom to the innocent.
The fear of the Lord is clean
and endures for ever;
the judgements of the Lord are true and righteous altogether.
More to be desired are they than gold,
more than much fine gold,
sweeter far than honey,
than honey in the comb.
By them is your servant enlightened,
and in keeping them there is great reward.

Second Reading   Matthew 19:27-30

Then Peter said in reply, 'Look we have left everything and followed you. What then will we have?'

Jesus said to them, 'Truly I tell you, at the renewal of all things, when the Son of Man is seated on the throne of his glory, you who have followed me will also sit on twelve thrones, judging the twelve tribes of Israel. And everyone who has left houses or brothers or sisters or father or mother or children or fields, for my name's sake, will receive a hundredfold, and will inherit eternal life. But many who are first will be last, and the last will be first.'

PICTURE – PONDER – PRAY – PROMISE

PRAYER

Lord,
let me pin all my hopes on you,
open my life to love you above all things.

Thoughts for private prayer

Praise God that those who serve him know true happiness
in this world and in heaven.

Thank him for the saints and martyrs of his church.

Pray for those who have divided loyalties,
and for those who find it hard to trust God.

If any would be first:
let them be last and servant of all.

O Lord, open our lips:
to praise you, the Saviour of all.

FIRST READING   Patrick Appleford (b. 1925)

O Lord, all the world belongs to you,
and you are always making all things new.
What is wrong you forgive
and the new life you give
is what's turning the world upside down.

O Lord, all the world belongs to you,
and you are always making all things new.
Send your Spirit on all
in your church whom you call
to be turning the world upside down.

SECOND READING   Matthew 20:1-16

'For the kingdom of heaven is like a land owner who went out
early in the morning to hire labourers for his vineyard. After
agreeing with the labourers for the usual daily wage, he sent them
into his vineyard. When he went out about nine o'clock, he saw
others standing idle in the marketplace; and he said to them, "You
also go into the vineyard, and I will pay you whatever is right."
   So they went. When he went out again about noon and about
three o'clock, he did the same. And about five o'clock he went out
and found others standing around; and he said to them, "Why are
you standing here idle all day?"
   They said to him, "Because no one has hired us."
   He said to them, "You also go into the vineyard."
   When evening came, the owner of the vineyard said to his
manager, "Call the labourers and give them their pay, beginning
with the last and then going to the first."
   When those hired about five o'clock came, each of them received
the usual daily wage. Now when the first came, they thought they
would receive more; but each of them also received the usual daily
wage. And when they received it, they grumbled against the

landowner, saying, "These last worked only one hour, and you have made them equal to us who have borne the burden of the day and the scorching heat."

But he replied to one of them, "Friend, I am doing you no wrong; did you not agree with me for the usual daily wage? Take what belongs to you and go; I choose to give to this last the same as I give to you. Am I not allowed to do what I choose with what belongs to me? Or are you envious because I am generous?"

So the last will be first, and the first will be last.'

PICTURE – PONDER – PRAY – PROMISE

PRAYER

Lord, your love and mercy
renews your world
and changes the very heart of human living:
help us to live out our faith
and to see life through the eyes of Jesus Christ.

Thoughts for private prayer

Thank God that Jesus is the true answer to life's needs.

Pray for insight and for courage to live as Jesus lived.

Pray for a just use and sharing of the wealth of the world.

Pray for those who are unemployed and lack money and the means to earn it.

Christ is the King of all the world:
and he shall reign for ever.

O Lord, open our lips:
to praise you with humble hearts.

FIRST READING   George Herbert (1593-1633)

Teach me, my God and King
in all things thee to see,
and what I do in any thing
to do it as for thee.

All may of thee partake:
nothing can be so mean
which with this tincture, 'for thy sake'.
will not grow bright and clean.

A servant with this clause
makes drudgery divine;
who sweeps a room as for thy laws
makes that and th'action fine.

This is the famous stone
that turneth all to gold;
for that which God doth touch and own
cannot for less be told.

SECOND READING   Matthew 20:20-27

Then the mother of the sons of Zebedee came to him with her sons,
and kneeling before him, she asked a favour of him. And he said to
her, 'What do you want?'

She said to him, 'Declare that these two sons of mine will sit, one
at your right hand and one at your left, in your kingdom.'

But Jesus answered, 'You do not know what you are asking. Are
you able to drink the cup that I am about to drink?'

They said to him, 'We are able.'

He said to them, 'You will indeed drink my cup, but to sit at my
right hand and at my left, this is not mine to grant, but it is for
those for whom it has been prepared by my Father.'

When the ten heard it, they were angry with the two brothers.

But Jesus called them to him and said, 'You know that the rulers of the Gentiles lord it over them, and their great ones are tyrants over them. It will not be so among you; but whoever wishes to be great among you must be your servant, and whoever wishes to be first among you must be your slave; just as the Son of Man came not to be served but to serve, and to give his life a ransom for many.'

PICTURE – PONDER – PRAY – PROMISE

PRAYER

Lord as you have served our needs
and won eternal life for us by dying on a cross,
may we serve all mankind in gratitude to you,
may simple gratitude our life command.

Thoughts for private prayer

Praise God for his death for us.

Pray to understand how death to selfishness
can mean true human greatness.

Pray for the gift of self-knowledge –
to do away with pride and to feel the love of God.

Whoever would be great:
must learn the joy of serving.

O Lord, open our lips:
to praise Christ with 'Hosanna!'

First Reading   Henry Vaughan (1622-1695)

Hark! how the children shrill and high Hosanna! cry.
Their joys provoke the distant sky,
where thrones and seraphims reply,
and their own angels shine and sing
in a bright ring:
such young, sweet mirth
makes heaven and earth
join in a joyful symphony.

Second Reading   Matthew 21:1-11

When they had come near Jerusalem and had reached Bethphage,
at the Mount of Olives, Jesus sent two disciples, saying to them,
'Go into the village ahead of you, and immediately you will find a
donkey tied, and a colt with her; untie them and bring them to me.
If anyone says anything to you, just say this, "The Lord needs
them." And he will send them immediately.' This took place to
fulfil what had been spoken through the prophet, saying,
    'Tell the daughter of Zion,
    Look your king is coming to you,
    humble, and mounted on a donkey,
    and on a colt, the foal of a donkey.'
The disciples went and did as Jesus had directed them; they
brought the donkey and the colt, and put their cloaks on them, and
he sat on them. A very large crowd spread their cloaks on the road,
and others cut branches from the trees and spread them on the
road. The crowds that went ahead of him and that followed were
shouting, 'Hosanna to the Son of David! Blessed is the one who
comes in the name of the Lord! Hosanna in the highest heaven!'

When he entered Jerusalem, the whole city was in turmoil, asking, 'Who is this?' The crowds were saying, 'This is the prophet Jesus from Nazareth in Galilee.'

PICTURE – PONDER – PRAY – PROMISE

PRAYER

We praise you Lord
as the people of Jerusalem praised you on the day of palms:
but do not let our praising turn to shouts of 'Crucify!'
May our faith and our love for you grow steadily more deep.

Thoughts for private prayer

Praise God that the people of Jerusalem
recognised Jesus on Palm Sunday.

Pray to be aware of his royal kingship in daily life.

Pray for the grace to be firm in faith.

Pray to be strong when the service of God
brings you against prejudice, hatred and opposition.

Hosanna to the Son of David!
blessed is he who comes in the name of the Lord.

O Lord, open our lips:
to sound your praise aloud.

FIRST READING   John Milton (1608-1674)

The Lord will come and not be slow,
his footsteps cannot err;
before him righteousness shall go,
his royal harbinger.

Truth from the earth like to a flower,
shall bud and blossom free;
and justice, from her heavenly bower,
bless all humanity.

Rise, God, judge thou the earth in might,
this wicked earth redress;
for thou art he who shalt by right
the nations all possess.

SECOND READING   Matthew 21:12-16

Then Jesus entered the temple and drove out all who were selling and buying in the temple, and he overturned the tables of the money changers and the seats of those who sold doves. He said to them, 'It is written, "My house shall be called a house of prayer"; but you are making it a den of robbers.'

The blind and the lame came to him in the temple, and he cured them. But when the chief priests and the scribes saw the amazing things that he did, and heard the children crying out in the temple, 'Hosanna to the Son of David', they became angry and said to him, 'Do you hear what these are saying?'

Jesus said to them, 'Yes; have you never read, "Out of the mouths of infants and nursing babies you have prepared praise for yourself"?'

PICTURE – PONDER – PRAY – PROMISE

PRAYER

The truth of your judgements is sure, O Lord our God;
grant us the grace to know the correction of your love,
inside ourselves and in the world about us.

Thoughts for private prayer

Pray for the gift of true repentance –
sorrow for sin and confidence in God's forgiving love.

Pray for the leaders of the nations,
for those who control commerce and industry,
for those who make and administer the law.

Pray for a world renewed and healed
by the merciful judgements of Christ.

Pray for the United Nations and all who work for peace.

Hosanna to the Son of David!
blessed is he who comes in the name of the Lord!

O Lord, open our lips:
and our minds to the greatness of your love.

FIRST READING   Vachel Lindsay (1879-1931)

Booth led boldly with his big brass drum –
(Are you washed in the blood of the Lamb?)
The saints smiled gravely and they said, 'He's come'.
(Are you washed in the blood of the Lamb?)
Walking lepers followed, rank on rank,
lurching bravos from the ditches dank,
drabs from the alleyways and drug fiends pale –
minds still passion-ridden, soul-powers frail –
vermin-eaten saints with mouldy breath,
unwashed legions with the ways of Death –
(Are you washed in the blood of the Lamb?)

SECOND READING   Matthew 21:23-32

When he entered the temple, the chief priests and the elders of the people came to him as he was teaching, and said, 'By what authority are you doing these things, and who gave you this authority?'

Jesus said to them, 'I will also ask you one question; if you tell me the answer, then I will also tell you by what authority I do these things. Did the baptism of John come from heaven, or was it of human origin?'

And they argued with one another, 'If we say, "From heaven," he will say to us, "Why then did you not believe him?" But if we say, "Of human origin," we are afraid of the crowd; for all regard John as a prophet.' So they answered Jesus, 'We do not know.'

And he said to them, 'Neither will I tell you by what authority I am doing these things.'

'What do you think? A man had two sons; he went to the first and said, "Son, go and work in the vineyard today." He answered, "I will not"; but later he changed his mind and went. The father went to the second and said the same; and he answered, "I go sir"; but he did not go. Which of the two did the will of his father?'

They said, 'The first.'

Jesus said to them, 'Truly I tell you, the tax collectors and the prostitutes are going into the kingdom of God ahead of you. For John came to you in the way of righteousness and you did not believe him, but the tax collectors and the prostitutes believed him; and even after you saw it, you did not change your minds and believe him.'

PICTURE – PONDER – PRAY – PROMISE

PRAYER

Grant, O Lord,
that we may honour you
not only with our lips
but in our lives,
opening ourselves to the service of your truth and love.

Thoughts for private prayer

Thank God that he loves you.

Thank God for his love of all mankind.

Pray for true discipleship in daily living.

Pray for all who are despised and rejected by society.

Pray for the grace to love others as God loves us.

For his wonderful love, let us bless the Lord:
let us live in the light of his grace.

O Lord, open our lips:
to acknowledge your justice and strength.

FIRST READING   Henry Alford (1810-1871)

For the Lord our God shall come,
and shall take his harvest home;
from his field shall purge away
all that doth offend, that day;
give his angels charge at last
in the fire the tares to cast,
but the fruitful ears to store
in his garner ever-more.

Then, thou Church triumphant, come,
raise the song of harvest home;
all be safely gathered in,
free from sorrow, free from sin,
there for ever purified,
in God's garner to abide:
come, ten thousand angels, come,
raise the glorious harvest-home!

SECOND READING   Matthew 21:33-43

'Listen to another parable. There was a landowner who planted a
vineyard, put a fence around it, dug a wine press in it, and built a
watchtower. Then he leased it to tenants and went to another
country. When the harvest time had come, he sent his slaves to the
tenants to collect his produce. But the tenants seized his slaves and
beat one, killed another, and stoned another. Again he sent other
slaves, more than the first; and they treated them in the same way.
Finally he sent his son to them, saying, "They will respect my son."
   But when the tenants saw the son, they said to themselves, "This
is the heir; come, let us kill him and get his inheritance." So they
seized him, threw him out of the vineyard, and killed him. Now
when the owner of the vineyard comes, what will he do to those
tenants?'

They said to him, 'He will put those wretches to a miserable death, and lease the vineyard to other tenants who will give him the produce at the harvest time.'

Jesus said to them, 'Have you never read in the scriptures: "The stone that the builders rejected has become the cornerstone; this was the Lord's doing, and it is amazing in our eyes"? Therefore I tell you, the kingdom of God will be taken away from you and given to a people that produces the fruits of the kingdom.'

PICTURE – PONDER – PRAY – PROMISE

PRAYER

God of creation,
nurture within our minds the truth that you are Lord
and we your stewards in the world.
May our lives reflect your justice in all its glory.

Thoughts for private prayer

Praise God for the beauty of creation.

Praise him, Lord of the universe.

Pray that mankind will cease to exploit
and learn to use the earth with reverence.

Pray for environmentalists
and for an end to the strife which kills the life of the world.

The earth is the Lord's and all that is in it:
He is the King of glory.

O Lord, open our lips:
to praise you will all our heart.

FIRST READING   Charles Wesley (1707-1788)

O for a heart to praise my God,
a heart from sin set free;
a heart that's sprinkled with the blood
so freely shed for me:

A humble, lowly, contrite heart,
believing, true, and clean,
which neither life nor death can part
from him that dwells within:

A heart in every thought renewed,
and full of love divine;
perfect and right and pure and good,
a copy, Lord, of thine.

SECOND READING   Matthew 22:1-14

Once more Jesus spoke to them in parables, saying: 'The kingdom
of heaven may be compared to a king who gave a wedding
banquet for his son. He sent his slaves to call those who had been
invited to the wedding banquet, but they would not come. Again
he sent other slaves, saying, "Tell those who have been invited:
Look, I have prepared my dinner, my oxen and my fat calves have
been slaughtered, and everything is ready; come to the wedding
banquet." But they made light of it and went away, one to his farm,
another to his business, while the rest seized his slaves, mistreated
them, and killed them. The king was enraged. He sent his troops,
destroyed those murderers, and burned their city. Then he said to
his slaves, "The wedding is ready, but those invited were not
worthy. Go therefore into the main streets, and invite everyone you
find to the wedding banquet." Those slaves went out into the
streets and gathered all whom they found, both good and bad; so
the wedding hall was filled with guests.

'But when the king came in to see the guests, he noticed a man there who was not wearing a wedding robe, and he said to him, "Friend, how did you get in here without a wedding robe?" And he was speechless. Then the king said to the attendants, "Bind him hand and foot, and throw him into the outer darkness, where there will be weeping and gnashing of teeth." For many are called, but few are chosen.'

PICTURE – PONDER – PRAY – PROMISE

PRAYER

Grant us, O Lord:
minds to understand you,
will-power to serve you,
and humility to know the weakness of our faith.

Thoughts for private prayer

Praise God that he invites all people to know and to love him.

Pray for the humility to know your sin and weakness
and great need of God.

Pray that the human race may find God
and receive the mercy he extends to all.

Pray for those who feel no need of God,
and for all who disregard his mercy and his forgiveness.

Make me a clean heart, O God:
and renew a right spirit within me.

O Lord, open our lips:
to praise you, creation's Lord.

FIRST READING   Robert Bridges (1844-1930)

All my hope on God is founded;
he doth still my trust renew.
Me through change and chance he guideth,
only good and only true.

Human pride and earthly glory,
sword and crown betray his trust;
what with care and toil he buildeth,
tower and temple, fall to dust.

From mankind to God eternal
sacrifice of praise be done,
high above all praises praising
for the gift of Christ his Son.
Christ doth call one and all:
ye who follow shall not fall.

SECOND READING   Matthew 22:15-22

Then the Pharisees went and plotted to entrap him in what he said.
So they sent their disciples to him, along with the Herodians,
saying, 'Teacher, we know that you are sincere, and teach the way
of God in accordance with truth, and show deference to no one; for
you do not regard people with partiality. Tell us, then, what you
think. Is it lawful to pay taxes to the emperor, or not?'

But Jesus, aware of their malice, said, 'Why are you putting me
to the test, you hypocrites? Show me the coin used for the tax.'
And they brought him a denarius. Then he said to them, 'Whose
head is this, and whose title?'

They answered, 'The emperor's.'

Then he said to them, 'Give therefore to the emperor the things that are the emperor's, and to God the things that are God's.'

When they heard this, they were amazed; and they left him and went away.

PICTURE – PONDER – PRAY – PROMISE

PRAYER

Help us, O Lord our God, to put you first in all we do;
give us the mind and wisdom of Jesus,
your Son and our true guide.

Thoughts for private prayer

Praise God for his wisdom given us by Jesus.

Pray to put God and his truth before all else in your life.

Pray for a right use of wealth in God's world and for those in need.

Pray for all caught up in fraud, dishonesty
and any kind of cheating.

Teach us, O Lord, the way of your laws:
that we may keep them to the end.

O Lord, open our lips:
to praise you, the God of the living.

FIRST READING   Thomas Olivers (1725-1799)

The God of Abraham praise
who reigns enthroned above,
ancient of everlasting days
and God of love:
to him uplift your voice,
at whose supreme command
from earth we rise and seek the joys
at his right hand.

The God who reigns on high,
the great archangels sing
and 'Holy, holy, holy!' cry,
'Almighty King!
Who was, and is the same,
and evermore shall be:
eternal Father, great I AM,
we worship thee.'

SECOND READING   Matthew 22:23-33

The same day some Sadducees came to him, saying there is no
resurrection; and they asked him a question, saying, 'Teacher,
Moses said, "If a man dies childless, his brother shall marry the
widow, and raise up children for his brother." Now there were
seven brothers among us; the first married, and died childless,
leaving the widow to his brother. The second did the same, so also
the third, down to the seventh. Last of all, the woman herself died.
In the resurrection, then, whose wife of the seven will she be? For
all of them had married her.'
    Jesus answered them, 'You are wrong, because you know neither
the scriptures nor the power of God. For in the resurrection they
neither marry nor are given in marriage, but are like angels in
heaven. And as for the resurrection of the dead, have you not read

what was said to you by God. "I am the God of Abraham, the God of Isaac, and the God of Jacob"? He is God not of the dead, but of the living.' And when the crowd heard it, they were astounded at his teaching.

PICTURE – PONDER – PRAY – PROMISE

PRAYER

Wisest King of all creation,
we worship you, eternal Father:
make us so fully aware of your greatness and love
that our lives shall be full of faith.

> *Thoughts for private prayer*
>
> Praise God – more alive than we can say,
> closer to us than we can understand.
>
> Pray for the wisdom that comes from simple devotion and trust.
>
> Pray for those so obsessed with cleverness
> hat they miss the truth of God.
>
> Pray for a reverence of life in us and in all creation,
> since God's life is in all he has made.

Eternal Father, great I AM:
we worship thee.

O Lord, open our lips:
to adore you with all our hearts.

FIRST READING   Timothy Rees (1874-1939)

God is love: and he enfoldeth all the world in one embrace;
with unfailing grasp he holdeth every child of every race.
And when human hearts are breaking under sorrow's iron rod,
then they find that self-same aching deep within the heart of God.

God is love: and though with blindness sin afflicts the souls of men,
God's eternal loving-kindness holds and guides them even then.
Sin and death and hell shall never over us final triumph gain;
God is love, so love for ever over the universe must reign.

SECOND READING   Matthew 23:34-40

When the Pharisees heard that he had silenced the Sadducees, they
gathered together, and one of them, a lawyer, asked him a question
to test him. 'Teacher, which commandment in the law is the
greatest?' He said to him, '"You shall love the Lord your God with
all your heart, and with all your soul and with all your mind." This
is the greatest and first commandment. And a second is like it:
"You shall love your neighbour as yourself." On these two
commandments hang all the law and the prophets.'

PICTURE – PONDER – PRAY – PROMISE

PRAYER

Lord, you have shown us in Jesus that you are love;
help us to love you deeply
and to love our neighbours as you love us.

Thoughts for private prayer

Thank God that he loves you – just as you are.

Pray to love others as God loves,
especially those most difficult to love.

Praise God that his love will win the world
despite all sin that blocks his love.

Pray for those unloved by the world,
especially the criminals, murderers and the worst of tyrants.

God is love and those who love:
are alive in the life of God.

O Lord, open our lips:
to praise you in spirit and in truth.

FIRST READING

Grant me, O Lord, a sense of proportion,
give me a spirit that laughs at my pride:
make me a knife that cuts clean to the motive,
bursting all bubbles of grandeur inside.

Good to look good, and nice to be noticed,
glad they don't know what I'm feeling within;
trouble, dear Lord, is you know all the answers,
how can you care for the mess that I am?

Want to be more than a bundle of clichés,
please make me real, and know what I'm worth;
hatred of self is as bad as complacency,
tune my dull wits to the voice of your love.

SECOND READING   Matthew 23:1-12

Then Jesus said to the crowds and to his disciples, 'The scribes and
the Pharisees sit on Moses' seat; therefore, do whatever they teach
you and follow it; but do not do as they do, for they do not practise
what they teach. They tie up heavy burdens, hard to bear, and lay
them on the shoulders of others; but they themselves are unwilling
to lift a finger to move them. They do all their deeds to be seen by
others; for they make their phylacteries broad and their fringes
long. They love to have the place of honour at banquets and the
best seats in the synagogues, and to be greeted with respect in the
market places, and to have people call them rabbi.

'But you are not to be called rabbi, for you have one teacher, and you are all students. And call no one your father on earth, for you have one Father – the one in heaven. Nor are you to be called Messiah. The greatest among you will be your servant. All who exalt themselves will be humbled, and all who humble themselves will be exalted.'

PICTURE – PONDER – PRAY – PROMISE

PRAYER

Lord, make us secure in your love;
deflate our pride and overcome our despair
that we may be truly children of your love.

Thoughts for private prayer

Thank God that he accepts and loves you – sins and all else.

Pray to be humble and ready to repent.

Pray to value yourself and other people
as God loves and values all.

Pray for those besotted with pride and pomposity.

Pray for those who are in despair and self-loathing.

Whoever exalt themselves will be humbled:
whoever humble themselves will be exalted. Alleluia!

O Lord, open our lips:
to praise and bless your name.

FIRST READING   Psalm 122:6-9

Pray for the peace of Jerusalem:
'May they prosper who love you.
Peace be within your walls
and quietness within your towers.
For my family and companions' sake
I pray for your prosperity.
Because of the house of the Lord our God,
I will seek to do you good.'

SECOND READING   Matthew 23:29-39

'Woe to you, scribes and Pharisees, hypocrites! For you build the
tombs of the prophets and decorate the graves of the righteous,
and you say, "If we had lived in the days of our ancestors, we
would not have taken part with them in shedding the blood of the
prophets." Thus you testify against yourselves that you are
descendants of those who murdered the prophets. Fill up, then, the
measure of your ancestors. You snakes, you brood of vipers! How
can you escape being sentenced to hell? Therefore I send you
prophets, sages, and scribes, some of whom you will kill and
crucify, and some you will flog in your synagogues and pursue
from town to town, so that upon you may come all the righteous
blood shed on earth, from the blood of righteous Abel to the blood
of Zechariah son of Barachiah, whom you murdered between the
sanctuary and the altar. Truly I tell you, all this will come upon this
generation.
    'Jerusalem, Jerusalem, the city that kills the prophets and stones
those who are sent to it! How often have I desired to gather your
children together as a hen gathers her brood under her wings,

and you were not willing! See, your house is left to you, desolate. For I tell you, you will not see me again until you say, "Blessed is the one who comes in the name of the Lord".'

PICTURE – PONDER – PRAY – PROMISE

PRAYER

O God of peace and love,
we pray for Jerusalem and for all the people of the Middle East;
grant peace and truth to all your human children
that they may learn to live in love.

Thoughts for private prayer

Thank God for Jesus whose death and resurrection in Jerusalem is the hope for the world.

Pray for peace and reconciliation
between Jew and Arab, between those at war,
between all who are divided by mistrust and hate.

Pray for any people whom you dislike and find difficult.

Blessed is he who comes in the name of the Lord!
Hosanna in the highest.

O Lord open our lips:
to praise and bless your name.

FIRST READING   Sir Walter Scott (1771-1832)

That day of wrath that dreadful day,
when heaven and earth shall pass away,
what power shall be the sinner's stay?
How shall he meet that dreadful day?

When shrivelling like a parched scroll,
the flaming heavens together roll;
when louder yet, and yet more dread,
swells the high trump that wakes the dead:

Oh! on that day, that wrathful day,
when man to judgement wakes from clay,
be thou, O Christ, the sinner's stay,
though heaven and earth shall pass away.

SECOND READING   Matthew 24:1-14

As Jesus came out of the temple and was going away, his disciples
came to point out to him the buildings of the temple. Then he
asked them, 'You see all these, do you not? Truly I tell you, not one
stone will be left here upon another; all will be thrown down.'
   When he was sitting on the Mount of Olives, the disciples came
to him privately, saying, 'Tell us, when will this be, and what will
be the sign of your coming and of the end of the age?'
   Jesus answered them, 'Beware that no one leads you astray. For
many will come in my name saying, "I am the Messiah!" and they
will lead many astray. And you will hear of wars and rumours of
wars; see that you are not alarmed; for this must take place, but the
end is not yet. For nation will rise against nation, and kingdom
against kingdom, and there will be famines and earthquakes in
various places: all this is but the beginning of the birthpangs.

'Then they will hand you over to be tortured and will put you to death, and you will be hated by all nations because of my name. Then many will fall away, and they will betray one another and hate one another. And many false prophets will arise and lead many astray. And because of the increase of lawlessness, the love of many will grow cold. But the one who endures to the end will be saved. And this good news of the kingdom will be proclaimed throughout the world, as a testimony to all the nations; and then the end will come.'

PICTURE – PONDER – PRAY – PROMISE

PRAYER

God of justice, God of truth;
teach us respect for you, and for your Law:
help us so to follow you through this world,
that we may live with you for ever.

> *Thoughts for private prayer*
>
> Praise God, whose justice shall be triumphant over every evil.
>
> Pray for the strength to live for God
> in the courage that we gain by our faith in Jesus.
>
> Pray for justice in human society,
> for judges, magistrates and police.
>
> Pray for the United Nations and for the respect of international law.

Whoever endures to the end:
shall live for all eternity.

O Lord, open our lips:
to adore you in love and in truth.

       Charles Wesley (1707-1788)

Come, thou long-expected Jesus,
born to set thy people free;
from our fears and sins release us;
let us find our rest in thee.

Israel's strength and consolation,
hope of all the earth, thou art;
dear desire of every nation,
joy of every longing heart.

Born thy people to deliver;
born a child and yet a king;
born to reign in us for ever;
now thy gracious Kingdom bring.

       Matthew 24:23-27

'Then if anyone says to you, "Look! Here is the Messiah!" or "There he is!" – do not believe it. For false Messiahs and false prophets will appear and produce great signs and omens, to lead astray, if possible, even the elect. Take note, I have told you beforehand. So, if they say to you, "Look! He is in the wilderness," do not go out. If they say, "Look! He is in the inner rooms," do not believe it. For as the lightning comes from the east and flashes as far as the west, so will be the coming of the Son of Man.'

PICTURE – PONDER – PRAY – PROMISE

PRAYER

Victorious Lord,
conqueror of death and evil,
may our hope and love be firmly fixed on you,
and on no other god or man.

Thoughts for private prayer

Thank God that Jesus is master of time and eternity.

Thank God that Jesus has overcome all evil
and that his kingship is for ever.

Pray to become ever more centred upon Jesus, hope of the world.

Pray for any who mislead others,
and for those who claim to know the mysteries of God.

Pray to be free of superstitions and of baseless fear and anxieties.

Christ is the King:
all may rejoice in him.

O Lord, open our lips:
awaken our minds to praise you.

FIRST READING   Philip Doddridge (1702-1751)

Ye servants of the Lord,
each for his coming wait,
observant of his heavenly word,
and watchful at his gate.

Let all your lamps be bright,
and trim the golden flame;
gird up your loins as in his sight,
for awesome is his name.

Watch! 'tis your Lord's command,
and while we speak, he's near;
mark the first signal of his hand,
and ready all appear.

Christ shall the banquet spread
with his own royal hand,
and raise each faithful servant's head
amid the angelic band.

SECOND READING   Matthew 25:1-13

'Then the kingdom of heaven will be like this. Ten bridesmaids
took their lamps and went to meet the bridegroom. Five of them
were foolish, and five were wise. When the foolish took their
lamps, they took no oil with them; but the wise took flasks of oil
with their lamps. As the bridegroom was delayed, all of them
became drowsy and slept. But at midnight there was a shout,
"Look! Here is the bridegroom! Come out to meet him." Then all
those bridemaids got up and trimmed their lamps. The foolish said
to the wise, "Give us some of your oil, for our lamps are going
out." But the wise replied, "No! there will not be enough for you or
for us; you had better go to the dealers and buy some for

yourselves." And while they went to buy it, the bridegroom came, and those who were ready went with him into the wedding banquet; and the door was shut. Later the other bridesmaids came also, saying, "Lord, lord, open to us." But he replied, "Truly I tell you, I do not know you." Keep awake therefore, for you know neither the day nor the hour.'

PICTURE – PONDER – PRAY – PROMISE

PRAYER

Grant us, O Lord, the grace to remain alert in your service,
to be ready to meet you in people and events of this life,
and to meet you at last in heaven.

Thoughts for private prayer

Pray for wisdom and stamina in living.

Pray for openness to the Holy Spirit.

Pray for those who ignore God and deny his reality.

Thank God that Jesus has revealed him
to all who desire to know him.

Keep awake in heart and mind:
for Christ is the master of space and time.

O Lord, open our lips:
and grant us thankful hearts.

FIRST READING

Only our God
can see the glory in each soul;
and only God
can know the gifts inside each life;
and only God
can use all we possess for good;
and only God
can fashion holiness from all;
and only we
to whom our lives are given,
can stop his love making us truly whole.

SECOND READING   Matthew 25:14-30

'For it is as if a man, going on a journey, summoned his slaves and
entrusted his property to them; to one he gave five talents, to
another two, to another one, to each according to his ability. Then
he went away. The one who had received the five talents went off
at once and traded with them. and made five more talents. In the
same way, the one who had the two talents made two more talents.
But the one who had received the one talent went off and dug a
hole in the ground and hid his master's money. After a long time
the master of those slaves came and settled accounts with them.
Then the one who had received the five talents came forward,
bringing five more talents, saying. "Master, you handed over to me
five talents; see, I have made five more talents." His master said to
him, "Well done, good and trustworthy slave; you have been
trustworthy in a few things, I will put you in charge of many
things; enter into the joy of your master." And the one with the
two talents also came forward, saying "Master, you handed over to
me two talents; see I have made two more talents." His master said
to him, "Well done, good and trustworthy slave; you have been
trustworthy in a few things, I will put you in charge of many

things; enter into the joy of your master." Then the one who had received the one talent also came forward, saying, "Master, I knew that you were a harsh man, reaping where you did not sow, and gathering where you did not scatter seed; so I was afraid, and I went and hid your talent in the ground. Here you have what is yours." But his master replied, "You wicked and lazy slave! You knew, did you, that I reap where I did not sow and gather where I did not scatter? Then you ought to have invested my money with the bankers, and on my return I would have received what was my own with interest. So take the talent from him, and give it to the one with the ten talents. For to all those who have, more will be given, and they will have an abundance; but from those who have nothing, even what they have will be taken away. As for this worthless slave, throw him into the outer darkness, where there will be weeping and gnashing of teeth."'

PICTURE – PONDER – PRAY – PROMISE

PRAYER

Father of all existence,
lover of all creation,
as you have given all for us in Christ,
may we give all we are to you, in gratitude.

Thoughts for private prayer

Thank God for life, for hope,
for gifts and talents that enrich your life.

Thank God that in the least of us, he can find greatness.

Pray to use every gift you have
to glorify God by the talents he has given you.

Pray for those who despise themselves,
those who despair,
those paralysed by hatred and fear,
those who are victims of drugs and other addictions.

God is our help and strength:
God's love our source of life.

O Lord, open our lips:
and our eyes, to see you in others.

FIRST READING   Philip Doddridge (1702-1751)

Jesus, my Lord, how rich thy grace,
how fair thy bounties shine!
What can my poverty bestow,
when all the worlds are thine?

But thou hast needy brethren here,
the partners of thy grace,
and wilt confess their humble names
before thy Father's face.

In them thou may'st be clothed and fed,
and visited and cheered,
and in their accents of distress
the Saviour's voice is heard.

Thy face with reverence and with love
I in thy poor would see;
O let me rather beg my bread,
than hold it back from thee.

SECOND READING   Matthew 25:31-46

'When the Son of Man comes in his glory, and all the angels with
him, then he will sit on the throne of his glory. All the nations will
be gathered before him, and he will separate people one from
another as a shepherd separates the sheep from the goats, and he
will put the sheep at his right hand and the goats at the left. Then
the king will say to those at his right hand, "Come, you that are
blessed by my Father, inherit the kingdom prepared for you from
the foundation of the world; for I was hungry and you gave me
food, I was thirsty and you gave me something to drink, I was a
stranger and you welcomed me, I was naked and you gave me
clothing, I was sick and you took care of me, I was in prison and

you visited me." Then the righteous will answer him, "Lord, when was it that we saw you hungry and gave you food, or thirsty and gave you something to drink? And when was it that we saw you a stranger and welcomed you, or naked and gave you clothing? And when was it that we saw you sick or in prison and visited you?" And the king will answer them, "Truly I tell you, just as you did it to one of the least of these who are the members of my family, you did it to me." Then he will say to those at his left hand, "You that are accursed, depart from me into the eternal fire prepared for the devil and his angels; for I was hungry and you gave me no food, I was thirsty and you gave me nothing to drink, I was a stranger and you did not welcome me, naked and you did not give me clothing, sick and in prison and you did not visit me."

Then they also will answer, "Lord, when was it that we saw you hungry or thirsty or a stranger or naked or sick or in prison, and did not take care of you?" Then he will answer them, "Truly I tell you, just as you did not do it to one of the least of these, you did not do it to me." And these will go away into eternal punishment, but the righteous into eternal life.'

PICTURE – PONDER – PRAY – PROMISE

PRAYER

O Lord,
you have taught us that care and love of others
is our way of serving you;
give us grace to keep this great command,
lest by selfishness we lose our very souls.

Thoughts for private prayer

Praise God for the directness of his love for all people.

Pray to show his love to others, and to care as he cares for all.

God says to us:
'Anything you do for others, you do for me.'

O Lord, open our lips:
to praise your eternal love.

FIRST READING   Matthew 26:1-13

When Jesus had finished saying all these things, he said to his
disciples, 'You know that after two days the passover is coming,
and the Son of Man will be handed over to be crucified.'
    Then the chief priests and the elders of the people gathered in
the palace of the high priest, who was called Caiaphas, and they
conspired to arrest Jesus by stealth and kill him. But they said, 'Not
during the festival, or there may be a riot among the people.'
    Now while Jesus was at Bethany in the house of Simon the leper,
a woman came to him with an alabaster jar of very costly ointment,
and she poured it on his head as he sat at the table.
    But when the disciples saw it, they were angry and said, 'Why
this waste? For this ointment could have been sold for a large sum,
and the money given to the poor.'
    But Jesus, aware of this, said to them, 'Why do you trouble the
woman? She has performed a good service for me. For you always
have the poor with you, but you will not always have me. By
pouring this ointment on my body she has prepared me for burial.
Truly I tell you, wherever this good news is proclaimed in the whole
world, what she has done will be told in remembrance of her.'

SECOND READING

She had no words, but they had many thousands
and could have loaded her with many more.
She had no theories, but they would have given her
two dozen ways you can address the Lord.

And she had not consulted the statistics,
she hadn't read the economics books,
she only knew that Jesus is Messiah,
the one who claimed her love for ever more.

PICTURE – PONDER – PRAY – PROMISE

PRAYER

God of grace and mercy,
we rejoice in your love and give thanks
that you accept the poor devotion of our lives.

Thoughts for private prayer

Praise God that he seeks from us, not cleverness, but love.

Thank him for opportunities to honour him,
and to serve him in our fellow human beings.

Pray for warmth of heart,
and for an ever-growing understanding of his love for us.

Pray for those who have no love
and have never been loved in their lives.

God is love, and those who abide in love:
abide in God and God in them.

O Lord, open our lips:
to praise your eternal love.

FIRST READING

I wished to make him wise and show him right;
the world is made of violence and sin,
I could have used his godly gifts to win
the human race as followers who fight.
I wanted him to claim Jerusalem
and pack the alien armies off to Rome
(he could throw thunderbolts to chase them home)
squeaking like porkers when the butchers come.
But he was all for love and mercy free
'Forgive your enemies and do them good.'
He thought the human race a brotherhood!
A much deluded man, that I now see!
He has to die; there's no way out of it,
this gentle Christ is destined for the pit!

SECOND READING   Matthew 26:14-25

Then one of the twelve, who was called Judas Iscariot, went to the
chief priests and said, 'What will you give me if I betray him to
you?' They paid him thirty pieces of silver. And from that moment
he began to look for an opportunity to betray him.

On the first day of Unleavened Bread the disciples came to Jesus,
saying, 'Where do you want us to make the preparations for you to
eat the Passover?'

He said, 'Go into the city to a certain man, and say to him, "The
Teacher says, My time is near; I will keep the Passover at your
house with my disciples."' So the disciples did as Jesus had
directed them, and they prepared the Passover meal.

When it was evening, he took his place with the twelve; and
while they were eating, he said, 'Truly I tell you, one of you will
betray me.' And they became greatly distressed and began to say
to him one after another, 'Surely not I, Lord?' He answered, 'The
one who has dipped his hand into the bowl with me will betray

me. The Son of Man goes as it is written of him, but woe to that one by whom the Son of Man is betrayed! It would have been better for that one not to have been born.'

Judas, who betrayed him, said, 'Surely not I, Rabbi?'

He replied, 'You have said so.'

PICTURE – PONDER – PRAY – PROMISE

PRAYER

Almighty Father,
have mercy upon us
when we betray the love you give to us:
help us to die to sin and pride,
and live for you in Christ.

Thoughts for private prayer

Praise and thank God for his forgiving love.

Praise him that he loves all people.

Confess and accept forgiveness for any sinful betrayals you have made of him and of the people you know.

Pray for all traitors, trust-breakers
and those who have let you down in any way.

O give thanks to the Lord for he is good:
great is his love, love without end.

O Lord, open our lips:
in unity of praise.

FIRST READING   An anonymous poem from the Middle Ages

Lo, here is fellowship,
one faith to hold,
one truth to speak,
one wrong to right,
one loving-cup to sip,
and to dip
in one dish faithfully,
as lambkins in one fold.
Either for other to suffer all thing,
one song to sing
in sweet accord and maken melody.
Right-so thou and I good-fellows be:
now God us save.

SECOND READING   Matthew 26:26-29

While they were eating, Jesus took a loaf of bread, and after blessing it he broke it, gave it to the disciples, and said, 'Take, eat; this is my body.'

Then he took a cup, and after giving thanks he gave it to them, saying, 'Drink from it, all of you; for this is my blood of the covenant, which is poured out for many for the forgiveness of sins. I tell you, I will never again drink of this fruit of the vine until that day when I drink it new with you in my Father's kingdom.'

PICTURE – PONDER – PRAY – PROMISE

PRAYER

Father of creation,
your Son has taught us that we are one fellowship in him;
help us to care for one another as you care for each of us.

Thoughts for private prayer

Thank God for Jesus
and for his gift to us of the sacrament of Holy Communion.

Pray that as the divided churches honour one Lord,
so may they grow into unity.

Pray that your own church congregation
may live in unity and love.

Pray for the other Christian churches in your neighbourhood.

Pray for the strength to forgive
and for the humility to be forgiven.

Jesus said, 'Love one another:
as I have loved you.'

O Lord, open our lips:
in faith and love and praise.

FIRST READING   Robert Herrick (1591-1674)

Lord, I am like to mistletoe,
which has no root, and cannot grow
or prosper, but by that same tree
it clings about; so I by thee.

What need I then to fear at all
so long as I about thee crawl?
But if that tree should fall and die,
tumble shall heaven, and down will I.

SECOND READING   Matthew 26:30-35

When they had sung the hymn, they went out to the Mount of
Olives.
   Then Jesus said to them, 'You will all become deserters because
of me this night; for it is written, "I will strike the shepherd, and
the sheep of the flock will be scattered." But after I am raised up, I
will go ahead of you to Galilee.'
   Peter said to him, 'Though all become deserters because of you, I
will never desert you.'
   Jesus said to him, 'Truly I tell you, this very night, before the
cock crows, you will deny me three times.'
   Peter said to him, 'Even though I must die with you, I will not
deny you.' And so said all the disciples.

PICTURE – PONDER – PRAY – PROMISE

PRAYER

Lord, take away our boastfulness,
deflate our pride and vanity,
teach us to remain faithful to you,
even when we do not understand all that you mean to us.

Thoughts for private prayer

Praise Christ that he was faithful,
even amidst the disciples' ignorant boasting.

Pray for grace to hold on to faith
in times of trouble and doubt.

Pray for those who find faith difficult,
and for those with no faith at all.

Pray for those who are full of unrealism and day-dreams.

Pray for those who have been so hurt by others
that they are filled with hatred and fear.

God is our strength and stay:
and he is our Saviour and King.

O Lord, open our lips:
and our hearts to the depths of your love.

FIRST READING

Come to Gethsemane and watch
the Saviour of the world in pain,
his suffering and his anxious prayer,
his sweat as others sleep in vain.

The deepest wound that burns his mind
is not the cross and vicious nails,
but apathy and fear and sleep
and love rejected and betrayed.

He fears the cross – for he's no sham –
he has a human heart like ours,
but open now to what must be,
the Christ is settled on his course.

This is the worst the world can do:
he knows himself to be alone,
and chooses freely love to serve –
the love of Father, Spirit, Son.

So now the triumph is complete
before the traitor's lying kiss,
before the priests and governor
have made their prudent sacrifice.

SECOND READING   Matthew 26:36-46

Then Jesus went with them to a place called Gethsemane; and he
said to his disciples, 'Sit here while I go over there and pray.' He
took with him Peter and the two sons of Zebedee, and began to be
grieved and agitated. Then he said to them, 'I am deeply grieved,
even to death; remain here, and stay awake with me.'

And going a little farther, he threw himself on the ground and prayed, 'My Father, if it is possible let this cup pass from me; yet not what I want but what you want.'

Then he came to the disciples and found them sleeping; and he said to Peter, 'So, could you not stay awake with me one hour? Stay awake and pray that you may not come into the time of trial; the spirit indeed is willing, but the flesh is weak.'

Again he went away for the second time and prayed, 'My Father, if this cannot pass unless I drink it, your will be done.'

Again he came and found them sleeping, for their eyes were heavy. So leaving them again, he went away and prayed for the third time, saying the same words. Then he came to the disciples and said to them, 'Are you still sleeping and taking your rest? See, the hour is at hand , and the Son of Man is betrayed into the hands of sinners. Get up, let us be going. See, my betrayer is at hand.'

PICTURE – PONDER – PRAY – PROMISE

PRAYER

O Love who has given all for me,
help me to give all to you.

> *Thoughts for private prayer*
>
> Praise God for the loving devotion of Jesus:
> his love of those who rejected him.
>
> Pray that you and the church of Jesus
> may follow his way to glory.
>
> Pray for traitors –
> especially any whom you think have betrayed you.

Love so amazing and divine:
demands my life, my soul, my all.

O Lord, open our lips:
to praise you, the suffering Christ.

FIRST READING   Psalm 42:1-7

As the deer longs for the water-brooks,
so longs my soul for you, O God.
My soul is athirst for God, athirst for the living God;
when shall I come to appear before the presence of God?
My tears have been my food day and night,
while all day long they say to me,
'Where now is your God?'
I pour out my soul when I think on these things:
how I went with the multitude
and led them into the house of God,
with the voice of praise and thanksgiving,
among those who keep holy day.
Why are you so full of heaviness, O my soul
and why are you so disquieted within me?
Put your trust in God;
for I will yet give thanks to him,
who is the help of my countenance, and my God.

SECOND READING   Matthew 26:47-56

While he was still speaking, Judas, one of the twelve, arrived; with
him was a large crowd with swords and clubs, from the chief
priests and the elders of the people. Now the betrayer had given
them a sign, saying, 'The one I will kiss is the man; arrest him.' At
once he came up to Jesus and said, 'Greetings, Rabbi!' and kissed
him.

Jesus said to him, 'Friend, do what you are here to do.' Then
they came and laid hands on Jesus and arrested him. Suddenly,
one of those with Jesus put his hand on his sword, drew it, and
struck the slave of the high priest, cutting off his ear. Then Jesus
said to him, 'Put your sword back into its place; for all who take
the sword will perish by the sword. Do you think that I cannot
appeal to my Father, and he will at once send me more than twelve

legions of angels? But how then would the scriptures be fulfilled, which say that it must happen in this way?' At that hour Jesus said to the crowds, 'Have you come out with swords and clubs to arrest me as though I were a bandit? Day after day I sat in the temple teaching, and you did not arrest me. But all this has taken place, so that the scriptures of the prophets may be fulfilled.' Then all the disciples deserted him and fled.

PICTURE – PONDER – PRAY – PROMISE

PRAYER

O God, as your son became the prisoner of sin
to save us all from sin,
may we be set free of every evil that corrupts our lives.

Thoughts for private prayer

Thank God for Jesus' steady faith
amidst the forces of evil and injustice.

Pray for all wrongfully imprisoned.

Pray for victims of racial and religious persecution.

Pray to be free of every habit that imprisons you in its grip of evil.

God is our refuge and strength:
a ready help in time of trouble.

O Lord, open our lips:
and our minds to your suffering for us.

First Reading   Matthew 26:57-68

Those who had arrested Jesus took him to Caiaphas the high priest,
in whose house the scribes and the elders had gathered. But Peter
was following him at a distance, as far as the courtyard of the high
priest; and going inside, he sat with the guards in order to see how
this would end. Now the chief priests and the whole council were
looking for false testimony against Jesus so that they might put him
to death, but they found none, though many false witnesses came
forward. At last two came forward and said, 'This fellow said, "I
am able to destroy the temple of God and to build it in three days".'
The high priest stood up and said, 'Have you no answer? What is it
that they testify against you?' But Jesus was silent. Then the high
priest said to him, 'I put you under oath before the living God, tell
us if you are the Messiah, the Son of God.'

Jesus said to him, 'You have said so. But I tell you, from now on
you will see the Son of Man seated at the right hand of Power and
coming on the clouds of heaven.'

Then the high priest tore his clothes and said, 'He has
blasphemed! Why do we still need witnesses? You have now heard
his blasphemy. What is your verdict?' They answered, 'He
deserves death.' Then they spat in his face and struck him; and
some slapped him, saying, 'Prophesy to us, you Messiah! Who is it
that struck you?'

Second Reading   Samuel Crossman (c. 1624-1684)

Why, what hath my Lord done?
What makes this rage and spite?
He made the lame to run,
he gave the blind their sight.
Sweet injuries!
Yet they at these
themselves displease,
and 'gainst him rise!

They rise, and needs will have
my dear Lord made away;
a murderer they save,
the Prince of Life they slay.
Yet cheerful he
to suffering goes,
that he his foes
from thence might free.

PICTURE – PONDER – PRAY – PROMISE

PRAYER

O Lord, who for us suffered cruel injustice
and the mockery of cowards,
may we be steadfast through the painfulness of life
to win with you the joy of heavenly life.

Thoughts for private prayer

Thank God for Jesus' steady faith
amidst lies, cruelty and mockery.

Pray for a faith like his.

Pray for all judges, magistrates
and those who have the lives and liberty of others in their power.

God's own true Son has suffered:
to bring true life to us.

O Lord, open our lips:
to proclaim our faith in you.

FIRST READING   John Gray (1866-1934)

A night alarm, a weaponed crowd;
one blow, and with the rest I ran.
I warmed my hands, and said aloud:
I never knew the man.

SECOND READING   Matthew 26:69-75

Now Peter was sitting outside in the courtyard. A servant-girl came to him and said, 'You also were with Jesus the Galilean.'

But he denied it before all of them, saying, 'I do not know what you are talking about.'

When he went out to the porch, another servant-girl saw him, and she said to the bystanders, 'This man was with Jesus of Nazareth.'

Again he denied it with an oath, 'I do not know the man.'

After a little while the bystanders came up and said to Peter, 'Certainly you are also one of them, for your accent betrays you.'

Then he began to curse, and he swore an oath, 'I do not know the man!' At that moment the cock crowed. Then Peter remembered what Jesus had said: 'Before the cock crows you will deny me three times.' And he went out and wept bitterly.

PICTURE – PONDER – PRAY – PROMISE

PRAYER

Oh! that it may be said of me,
'Surely thy speech betrayeth thee,
thou hast been with Jesus of Galilee,
with Jesus of Galilee.'

Thoughts for private prayer

Thank God that out of Peter's failure
God brought repentance, renewal,
new life and faithfulness to a martyr's death.

Remember your own acts of cowardice,
seeking forgiveness and new faithfulness to Jesus.

Pray for anyone you feel you have ever let down or neglected.

Pray for victims of the human race's faithlessness:
the homeless, the oppressed, the starving,
the neglected (especially children).

Pray that the Church of Jesus will be faithful to the Gospel,
despite unpopularity and misunderstanding.

Christ has endured the cross, ignoring its disgrace:
and he reigns in heaven for ever more.

O Lord, open our lips:
to adore your suffering for us.

FIRST READING   Matthew 27:1-10

When morning came, all the chief priests and the elders of the
people conferred together against Jesus in order to bring about his
death. They bound him, led him away, and handed him over to
Pilate the governor.

When Judas, his betrayer, saw that Jesus was condemned, he
repented and brought back the thirty pieces of silver to the chief
priests and the elders. He said, 'I have sinned by betraying
innocent blood.'

But they said, 'What is that to us? See to it yourself.'

Throwing down the pieces of silver in the temple, he departed;
and he went and hanged himself.

But the chief priests, taking the pieces of silver, said, 'It is not
lawful to put them into the treasury, since they are blood money.'
After conferring together, they used them to buy the potter's field
as a place to bury foreigners. For this reason that field has been
called the Field of Blood to this day. Then was fulfilled what had
been spoken through the prophet Jeremiah, 'And they took the
thirty pieces of silver, the price of the one on whom a price had
been set, on whom some of the people of Israel had set a price, and
they gave them for the potter's field, as the Lord commanded me.'

SECOND READING

'Forgive me Lord,' he could have prayed
on this most black of days,
'For thirty silver pieces, Lord,
I sold your life away.'

And Jesus, even on his cross,
could set him free from sin,
but Judas feared forgiveness more
than guilt and hate within.

To find our God a soul requires,
not perfectness of life,
but openness that owns the need
for healing from sin's blight.

Because he wished to master Christ
and chose the way of pride
he sealed himself away from love,
condemned himself and died.

PICTURE – PONDER – PRAY – PROMISE

PRAYER

Great God of love and Father of creation,
make us as ready to repent as you are to forgive.

Thoughts for private prayer

Adore and praise God's endless mercy and forgiveness.

Pray for the grace to repent and to know your need of forgiveness.

Pray for those who condemn themselves and hate their own lives.

Pray for the Samaritans and all who seek to help others in despair.

O give thanks to the Lord for he is good:
for his mercy endures for ever!

O Lord open our lips:
and open our hearts to your weakness.

FIRST READING   Matthew 27:11-26

Now Jesus stood before the governor; and the governor asked him,
'Are you the King of the Jews?' Jesus said, 'You say so.' But when
he was accused by the chief priests and elders, he did not answer.
Then Pilate said to him, 'Do you not hear how many accusations
they make against you?' But he gave him no answer, not even to a
single charge, so that the governor was greatly amazed.

Now at the festival the governor was accustomed to release a
prisoner for the crowd, anyone whom they wanted. At that time
they had a notorious prisoner, called Jesus Barabbas. So after they
had gathered, Pilate said to them, 'Whom do you want me to
release for you, Jesus Barabbas or Jesus who is called the Messiah?'
For he realized that it was out of jealousy that they had handed
him over. While he was sitting on the judgment seat, his wife sent
word to him, 'Have nothing to do with that innocent man, for
today I have suffered a great deal because of a dream about him.'

Now the chief priests and the elders persuaded the crowds to
ask for Barabbas and to have Jesus killed. The governor again said
to them, 'Which of the two do you want me to release for you?'

And they said, 'Barabbas.'

Pilate said to them, 'Then what should I do with Jesus who is
called the Messiah?'

All of them said, 'Let him be crucified!'

Then he asked, 'Why, what evil has he done?'

But they shouted all the more, 'Let him be crucified!'

So when Pilate saw that he could do nothing, but rather that a
riot was beginning, he took some water and washed his hands
before the crowd, saying, 'I am innocent of this man's blood, see to
it yourselves.'

Then the people as a whole answered, 'His blood be on us and
on our children!' so he released Barabbas for them; and after
flogging Jesus, he handed him over to be crucified.

SECOND READING

Another day, another trial sat Pilate on his throne,
and warily he sent them off to prison or to home,
and some he sent to crucify to save the peace of Rome.

Another man, a foolish man of a religious turn,
they said he called himself a god and made the rabble burn
with wrong ideas and nasty thoughts to shake the power of Rome.

Shrewd Pilate looked him in the eye and heard the locals say
the man was bad and troublesome and getting in their way.
And though the case was clearly weak he had to earn his pay
so washed his hands and went to dine and had Christ put away.

PICTURE – PONDER – PRAY – PROMISE

PRAYER

O God of truth,
help us live by truth and never murder you with lies.

> *Thoughts for private prayer*

> Pray for all who wield power,
> especially those with power to take the lives of others.

> Pray for truth and justice in the world –
> especially where there is oppression.

> Praise God that the truth shall never die.

Jesus said, 'I am the way, the truth and the life:
no one comes to the Father, but by me.'

O Lord, open our lips:
and our minds to the needs of your world.

FIRST READING   Matthew 27:27-34

Then the soldiers of the governor took Jesus into the governor's
headquarters, and they gathered the whole cohort around him.
They stripped him and put a scarlet robe on him, and after
twisting some thorns into a crown, they put it on his head. They
put a reed in his right hand and knelt before him and mocked him,
saying, 'Hail, King of the Jews!' They spat on him, and took the
reed and struck him on the head. After mocking him, they stripped
him of the robe and put his own clothes on him. Then they led him
away to crucify him.

As they went out, they came upon a man from Cyrene named
Simon; they compelled this man to carry his cross. And when they
came to a place called Golgotha (which means Place of a Skull),
they offered him wine to drink, mixed with gall; but when he
tasted it, he would not drink it.

SECOND READING

Picked up the timber, heaved him on upward,
into the Calvary mess I was thrown,
smelling the dust and the sweating and jeering,
picked out because I'd been easy to grasp.

Suddenly noticed, I had his perspective,
looked at the crowd from under his cross,
saw all the cowardice, tasted the hatred,
felt the cold thrill as they lusted for blood.

Now I was under the cross, I could see it.
I was his courtier, carried his throne,
it was his death, it was also his crowning,
love was unbroken and winning the world.

PICTURE – PONDER – PRAY – PROMISE

PRAYER

Praise to you, Lord Christ,
who allowed Simon of Cyrene to share the burden of your cross:
teach us to share the burdens of the weak
and so to share your love for all mankind.

Thoughts for private prayer

Praise God who allows us
to have a part in serving him in other people.

Pray for sensitivity to the real needs of others.

Pray that the nations of the world
may build true peace by caring for each other.

Bear one another's burdens:
and so fulfil the law of Christ.

O Lord, open our lips:
and our eyes to look at your cross.

FIRST READING   Matthew 27:38-54

Then two bandits were crucified with him, one on his right and
one on his left. Those who passed by derided him, shaking their
heads and saying, 'You who would destroy the temple and build it
in three days, save yourself! If you are the Son of God, come down
from the cross.' In the same way the chief priests also, along with
the scribes and elders, were mocking him, saying, 'He saved
others; he cannot save himself. He is the King of Israel; let him
come down from the cross now, and we will believe in him. He
trusts in God; let God deliver him now, if he wants to; for he said,
"I am God's Son."' The bandits who were crucified with him also
taunted him in the same way.

From noon on, darkness came over the whole land until three in
the afternoon. And about three o'clock Jesus cried with a loud
voice, 'Eli, Eli, lema sabachthani?' that is, 'My God, my God, why
have you forsaken me?'

When some of the bystanders heard it, they said, 'This man is
calling for Elijah.' At once one of them ran and got a sponge, filled
it with sour wine, put it on a stick, and gave it to him to drink. But
the others said, 'Wait, let us see whether Elijah will come to save
him.' Then Jesus cried again with a loud voice and breathed his last.
At that moment the curtain of the temple was torn in two, from top
to bottom. The earth shook, and the rocks were split. The tombs
also were opened, and many bodies of the saints who had fallen
asleep were raised. After his resurrection they came out of the
tombs and entered the holy city and appeared to many. Now when
the centurion and those with him, who were keeping watch over
Jesus, saw the earthquake and what took place, they were terrified
and said, 'Truly this man was God's Son!'

SECOND READING   Isaac Watts (1674-1748)

When I survey the wondrous cross
on which the Prince of Glory died,
my richest gain I count but loss,
and pour contempt on all my pride.

Forbid it, Lord, that I should boast
save in the death of Christ, my God;
all the vain things that charm me most,
I sacrifice them to his blood.

See from his head, his hands, his feet,
sorrow and love flow mingling down;
did e'er such love and sorrow meet,
or thorns compose so rich a crown?

Were the whole realm of nature mine,
that were an offering far too small;
love so amazing, so divine,
demands my soul, my life, my all.

PICTURE – PONDER – PRAY – PROMISE

PRAYER

Lord, in the desolation of the cross we see your love proclaimed:
In the helplessness of death you have saved the world.
Alleluia!

Thoughts for private prayer

Praise God that in the moment of defeat,
Christ has destroyed the power of death.

Pray for the dying and the departed,
especially your own loved ones.

Pray for those who fear dying.

Pray for hospices and all who minister to the terminally ill.

In the midst of death we find life:
for Christ Jesus has conquered the grave.

O Lord, open our lips:
to praise your death divine.

FIRST READING

Folded the healer's hands,
silent the teacher's voice,
shrouded the body stilled by death,
the agony is passed.

No work, no struggle now,
he has let go his task
in space and time: now soon can dawn
a new created life.

Through loss of human hope
he gained the hope divine
and by his death, for all mankind,
completes our road to God.

SECOND READING   Matthew 27:55-66

Many women were also there, looking on from a distance; they
had followed Jesus from Galilee and had provided for him. Among
them were Mary Magdalene, and Mary the mother of James and
Joseph, and the mother of the sons of Zebedee.

When it was evening, there came a rich man from Arimathea,
named Joseph, who was also a disciple of Jesus. He went to Pilate
and asked for the body of Jesus; then Pilate ordered it to be given
to him. So Joseph took the body and wrapped it in a clean linen
cloth and laid it in his own new tomb, which he had hewn in the
rock. He then rolled a great stone to the door of the tomb and went
away. Mary Magdalene and the other Mary were there, sitting
opposite the tomb.

The next day, that is, after the day of Preparation, the chief
priests and the Pharisees gathered before Pilate and said, 'Sir, we
remember what that impostor said while he was still alive, "After
three days I will rise again" Therefore command the tomb to be

made secure until the third day; otherwise his disciples may go and steal him away and tell the people, "He has been raised from the dead," and the last deception would be worse than the first.'

Pilate said to them, 'You have a guard of soldiers; go, make it as secure as you can.'

So they went with the guard and made the tomb secure by sealing the stone.

PICTURE – PONDER – PRAY – PROMISE

PRAYER

Hope and light of the world;
we rest in your peace,
and trust in your love for ever.

Thoughts for private prayer

Thank God for Jesus
and for his faithfulness to God and to our human need.

Pray for true peace of heart and strength of faith.

Pray for those who have no peace,
for those gripped by anxiety,
for those who live in daily fear of violence and murder.

In the midst of death we find life:
for Christ has conquered the grave.

O Lord, open our lips:
to sing your Easter praise!

FIRST READING   John Mason Neale (1818-1866)

The day of Resurrection!
Earth, tell it out abroad;
the Passover of gladness,
the Passover of God!
From death to life eternal,
from earth unto the sky,
our Christ hath brought us over
with hymns of victory.

Now let the heavens be joyful,
and earth her song begin,
the round world keep high triumph,
and all that is therein;
let all things seen and unseen
their notes of gladness blend,
for Christ the Lord hath risen,
our joy that hath no end!

SECOND READING   Matthew 28:1-10

After the sabbath, as the first day of the week was dawning, Mary
Magdalene and the other Mary went to see the tomb. And
suddenly there was a great earthquake; for an angel of the Lord,
descending from heaven, came and rolled back the stone and sat
on it. His appearance was like lightning, and his clothing white as
snow. For fear of him the guards shook and became like dead men.
But the angel said to the women, 'Do not be afraid; I know that
you are looking for Jesus who was crucified. He is not here; for he
has been raised, as he said. Come, see the place where he lay. Then
go quickly and tell his disciples, "He has been raised from the
dead, and indeed he is going ahead of you to Galilee; there you
will see him." This is my message for you.' So they left the tomb
quickly with fear and great joy, and ran to tell his disciples.

Suddenly Jesus met them and said, 'Greetings!' And they came to him, took hold of his feet, and worshipped him. Then Jesus said to them, 'Do not be afraid; and tell my brothers to go to Galilee; there they will see me.'

PICTURE – PONDER – PRAY – PROMISE

PRAYER

We praise, adore and bless your love, O God;
you have destroyed the power of death,
and given us eternal life,
Alleluia!

> *Thoughts for private prayer*
>
> Praise God for the triumph of Jesus.
>
> Adore him for the victory of love.
>
> Thank him for hope, for life, for everything.
>
> Pray that all the peoples of the world shall come to know his Resurrection life.

The Lord is risen:
he is risen indeed, Alleluia!

O Lord, open our lips:
to share the good news of your Resurrection!

FIRST READING   Edward Burns (b. 1938)

We have a Gospel to proclaim,
good news for all in all the earth;
The gospel of a Saviour's name:
we sing his glory, tell his worth.

Tell of his death at Calvary,
hated by those he came to save,
in lonely suffering on the cross;
for all he loved his life he gave.

Tell of that glorious Easter morn:
empty the tomb for he was free.
he broke the power of death and hell
that we might share his victory.

SECOND READING   Matthew 28:16-20

Now the eleven disciples went to Galilee, to the mountain to which
Jesus had directed them. When they saw him, they worshipped
him; but some doubted. And Jesus came and said to them, 'All
authority in heaven and on earth has been given to me. Go
therefore and make disciples of all nations, baptizing them in the
name of the Father and of the Son and of the Holy Spirit, and
teaching them to obey everything that I have commanded you.
And remember, I am with you always, to the end of the age.'

PICTURE – PONDER – PRAY – PROMISE

PRAYER

O Lord, you have entrusted to your Church
the spreading of the good news of Jesus and his Resurrection:
help us to be true to his command and bring others to faith in him.

> *Thoughts for private prayer*
>
> Thank God for Jesus, conquerer of sin and death.
>
> Pray to be able in word and action
> to help others to understand the truth of our faith
> and feel for themselves the love of God.
>
> Pray for all evangelists,
> that they may be effective in their work.

The Lord is risen:
he is risen indeed, Alleluia!

ACKNOWLEDGEMENTS

All Scripture quotations are taken from *The New Revised Standard Version* of the Bible, copyright © 1989 by the Division of Christian Education of the National Council of the Churches of Christ in the USA. Used by permission. All rights reserved.

The publishers also wish to express their gratitude to the following for permission to reproduce copyright material in this publication:

Canon E. J. Burns for the words of the hymn *We have a gospel to proclaim*.

Josef Weinberger Limited, 12-14 Mortimer Street, London W1N 7RD for the words of the hymn *O Lord, all the world belongs to you* by Patrick Appleford © 1965 Josef Weinberger Ltd.

All unattributed readings are by Richard Garrard and are the copyright of Kevin Mayhew Ltd.

Every effort has been made to trace the owners of copyright material included in this publication and we hope that no copyright has been infringed. Pardon is sought and apology made if the contrary be the case, and a correction will be made in any reprint of this book.